BOOK 4

MW01485637

11 Piano Arrangements of Traditional Favorites
Arranged by Melody Bober & Robert D. Vandall

In the *Play HYMNS* series, pianists young and old will find accessible arrangements of beloved hymns, which are a continuous source of inspiration and an important part of worship services.

It is best for piano students to observe the rhythms as notated, but these may be adjusted later to match what they have heard at church.

The joy found in learning these arrangements will result in performers who want to continue to *Play HYMNS*.

Alfred Music Publishing Co., Inc.
P.O. Box 10003
Van Nuys, CA 91410-0003
alfred.com

ISBN-10: 0-7390-7741-4
ISBN-13: 978-0-7390-7741-2

All Hail the Power of Jesus' Name

Words by Edward Perronet
Music by Oliver Holden
Arr. Melody Bober

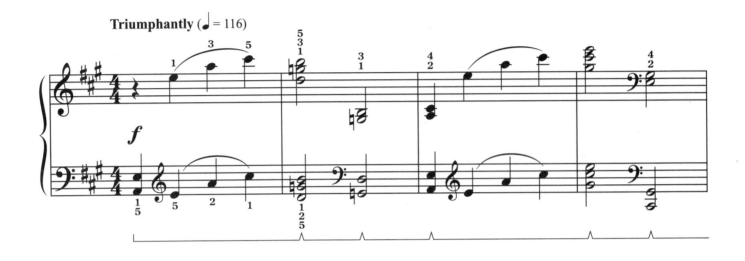

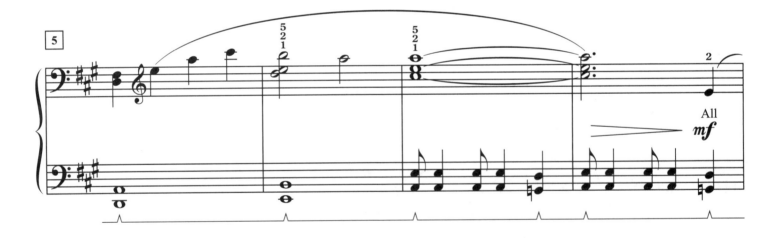

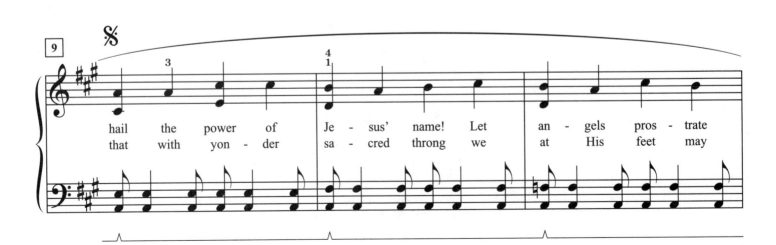

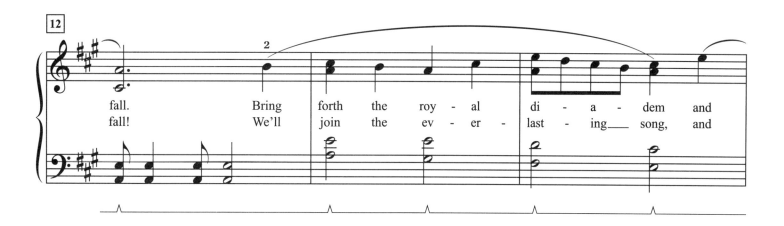

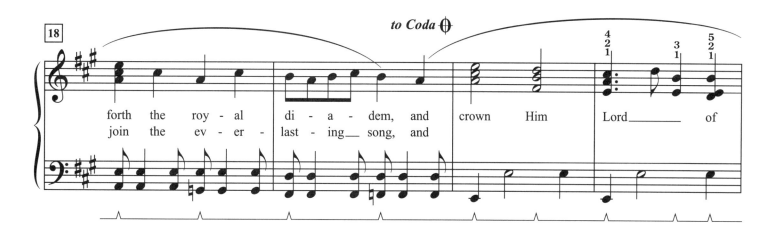

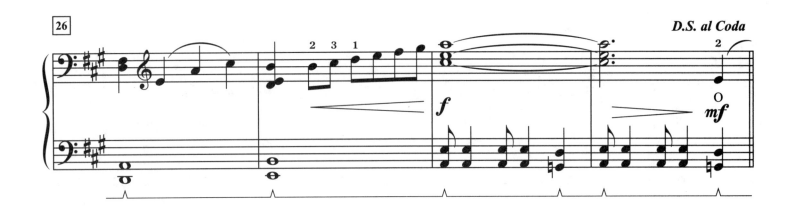

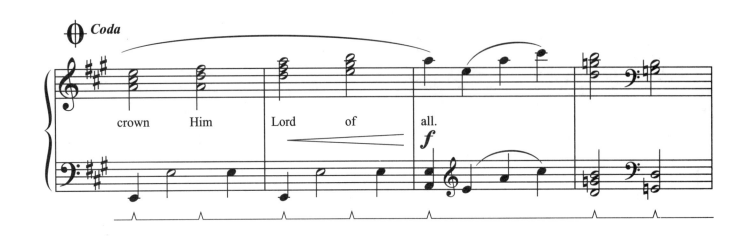

crown Him Lord of all.

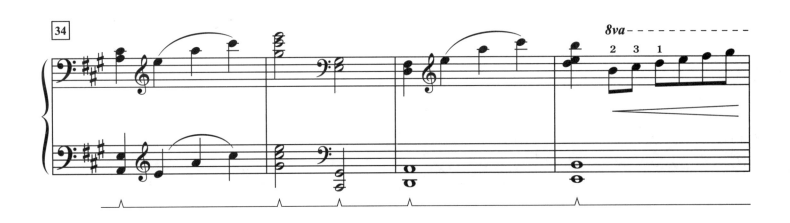

Amazing Grace! How Sweet the Sound

Words by John Newton
Music from *Virginia Harmony*
Arr. Robert D. Vandall

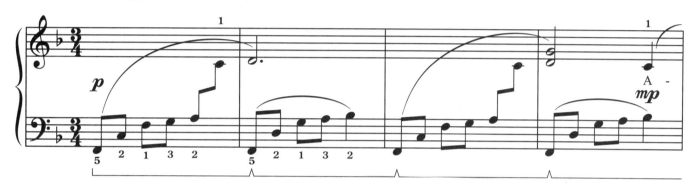

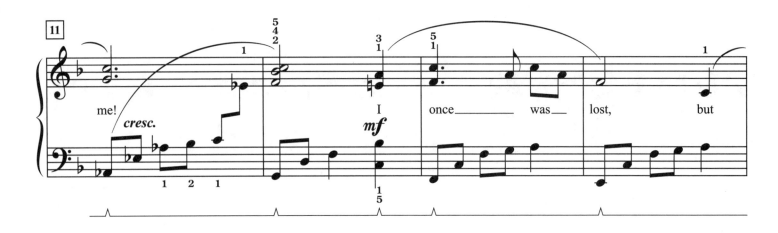

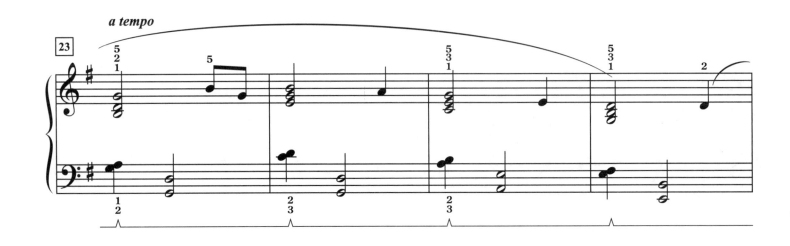

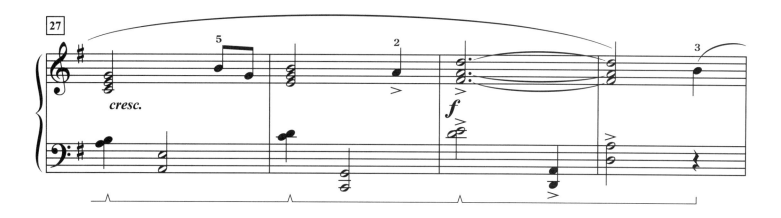

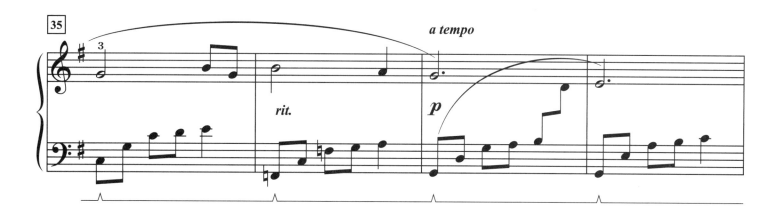

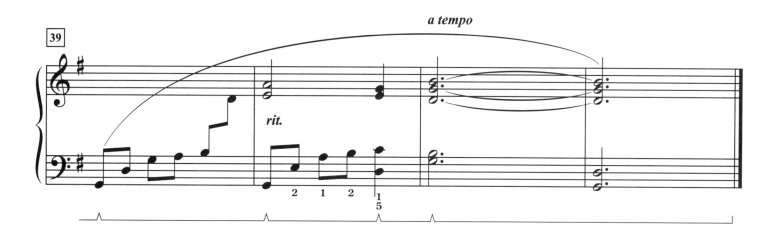

Beneath the Cross of Jesus

Words by Elizabeth C. Clephane
Music by Frederick C. Maker
Arr. Melody Bober

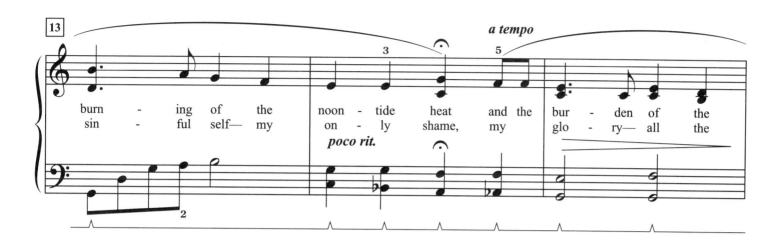

burn - ing of the noon - tide heat and the bur - den of the

sin - ful self— my on - ly shame, my glo - ry— all the

day.

cross.

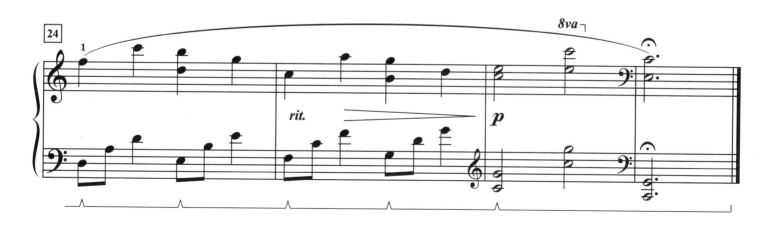

I've Got Peace like a River

Spiritual
Arr. Robert D. Vandall

Flowing and expressive (♩ = ca. 108)

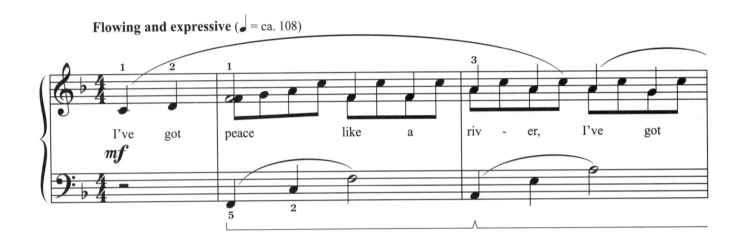

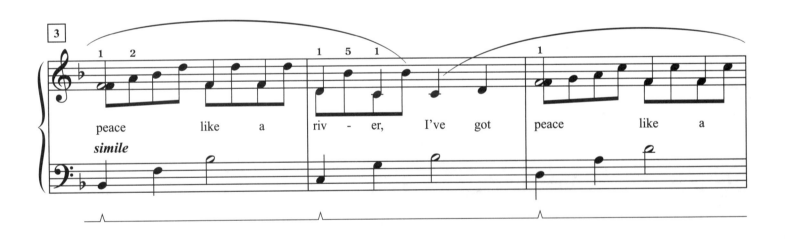

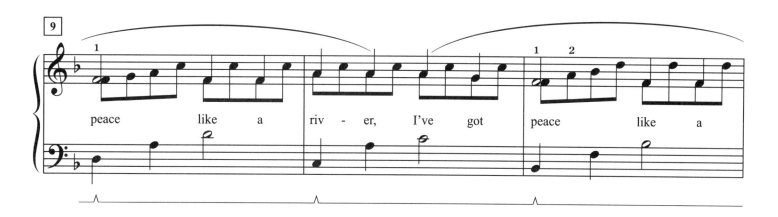

peace like a riv - er, I've got peace like a

riv - er, I've got peace like a riv - er in my

soul.

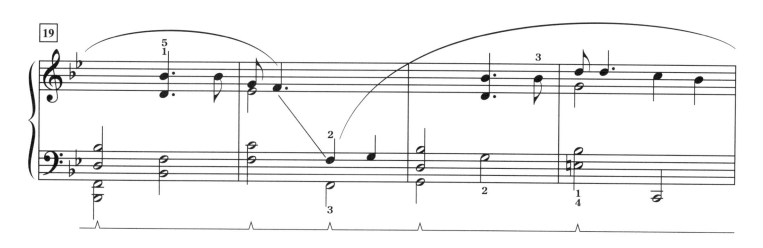

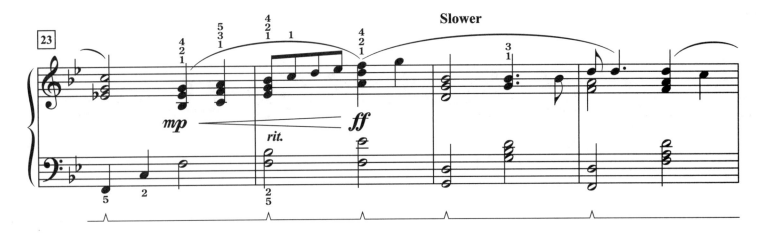

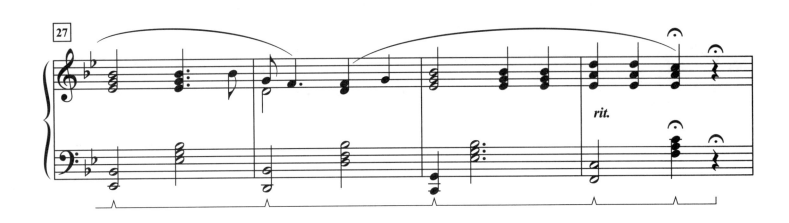

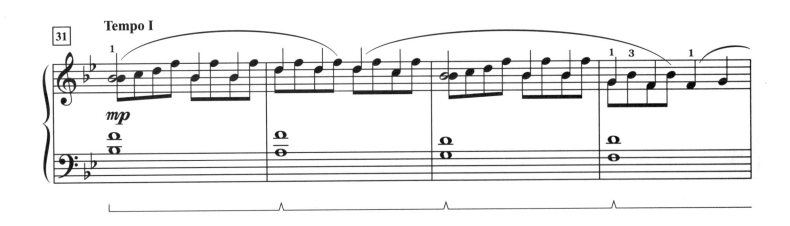

Joyful, Joyful, We Adore Thee

Words by Henry van Dyke
Music by Ludwig van Beethoven
Arr. Robert D. Vandall

Joy - ful, joy - ful, we a - dore Thee, God of glo - ry,

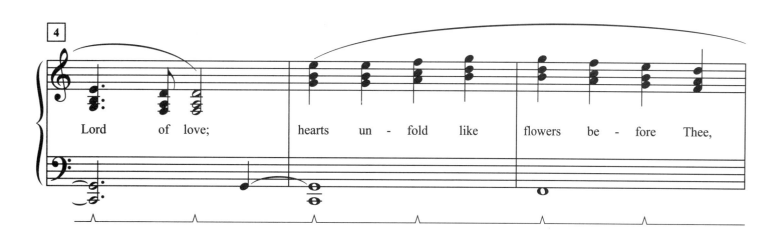

Lord of love; hearts un - fold like flowers be - fore Thee,

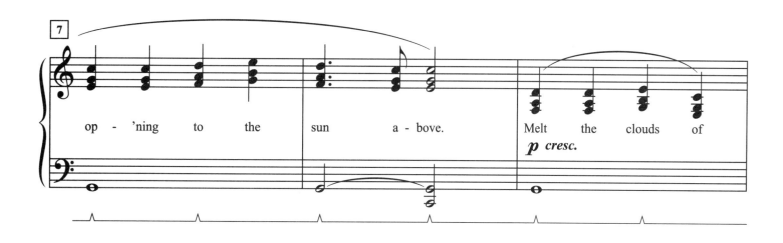

op - 'ning to the sun a - bove. Melt the clouds of

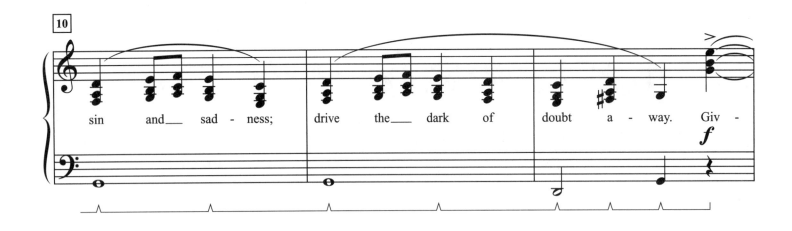

sin and__ sad - ness; drive the__ dark of doubt a - way. Giv -

er of im - mor - tal glad - ness, fill us with the light of day!

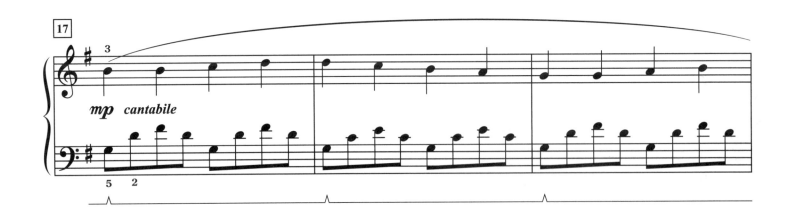

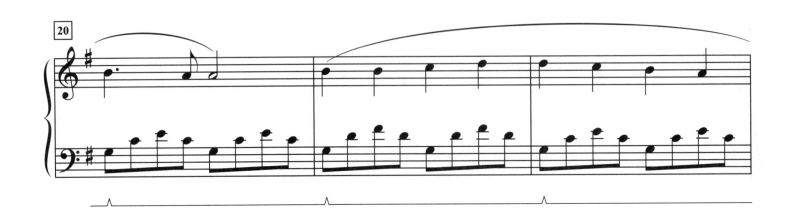

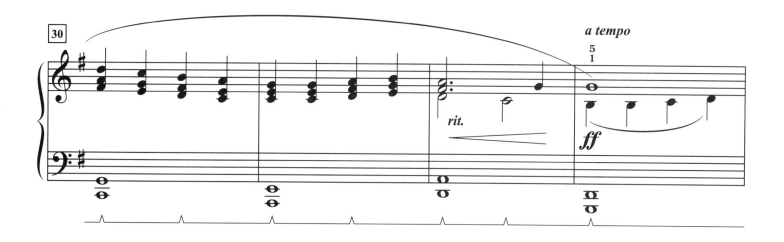

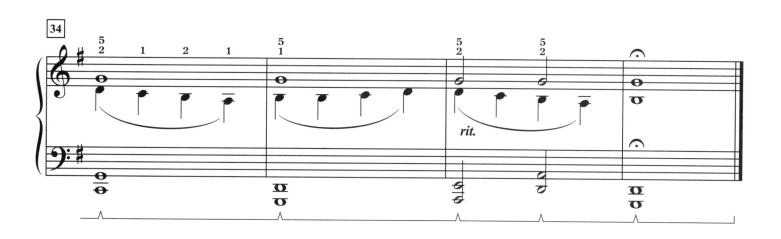

Kum Ba Yah

Afro-American spiritual
Arr. Robert D. Vandall

Moderately slow (♩ = ca. 50)

Kum ba yah, my Lord, kum ba yah. Kum ba

yah, my Lord, kum ba yah. Kum ba

yah, my Lord, kum ba yah. Oh,

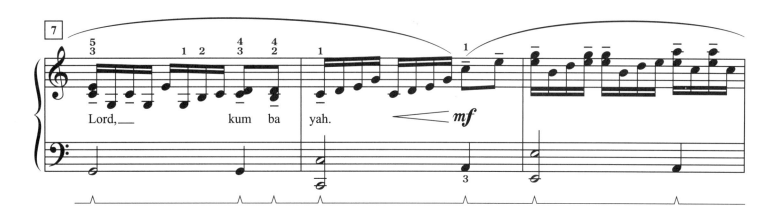

Lord,___ kum ba yah.

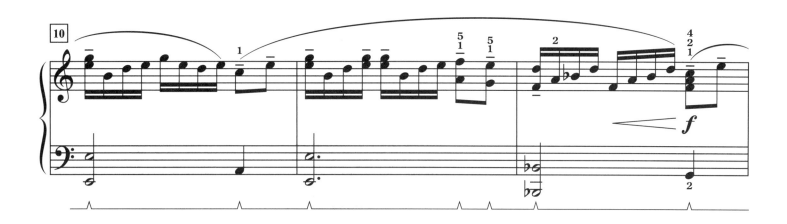

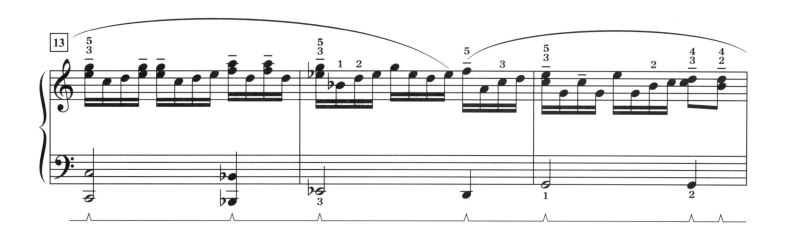

Just As I Am

Words by Charlotte Elliott
Music by William B. Bradbury
Arr. Melody Bober

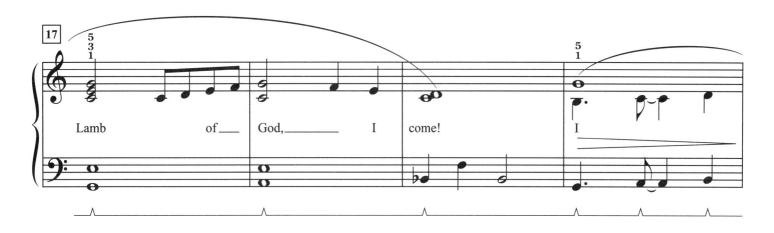

Lamb of ___ God, ____ I come!

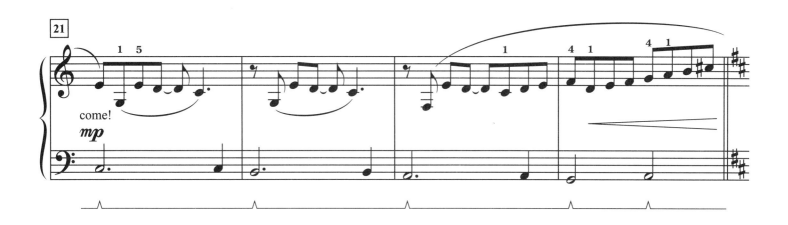

come!

mp

mf

Slower

mp

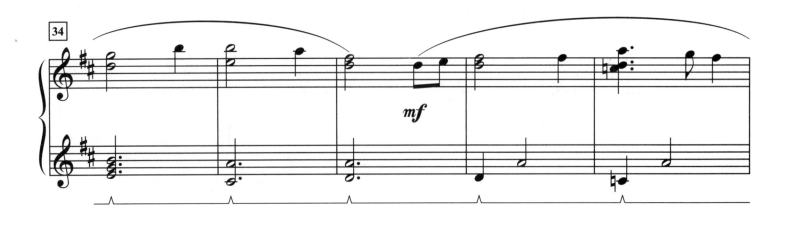

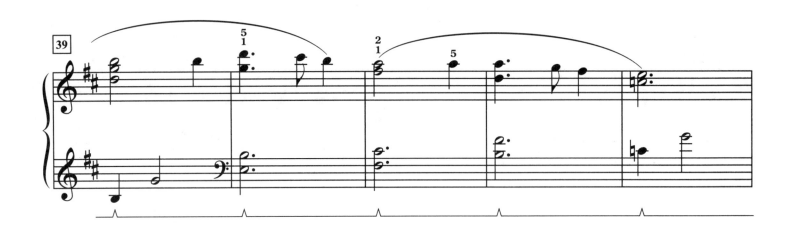

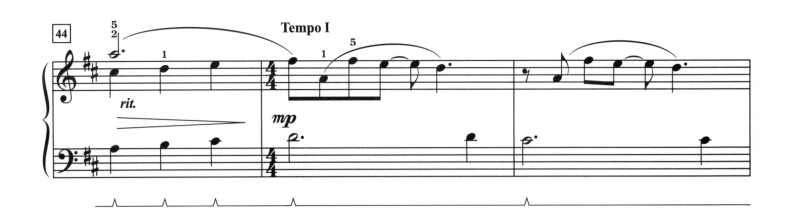

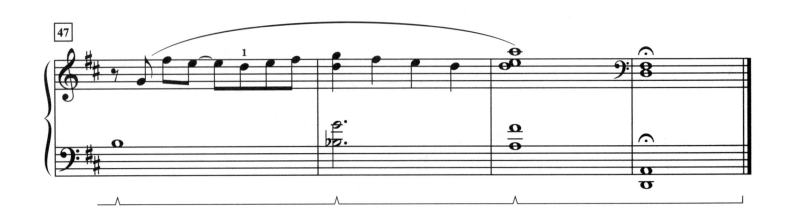

Rock of Ages, Cleft for Me

Words by Augustus M. Toplady
Music by Thomas Hastings
Arr. Melody Bober

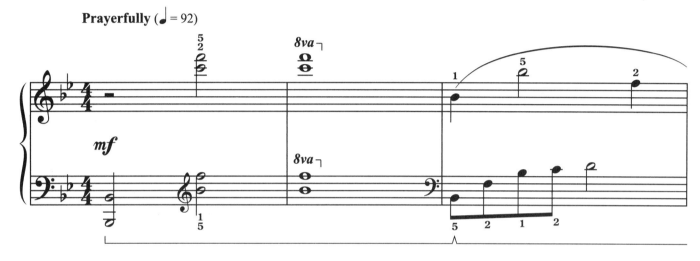

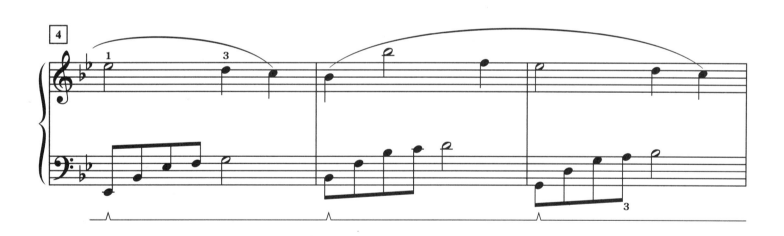

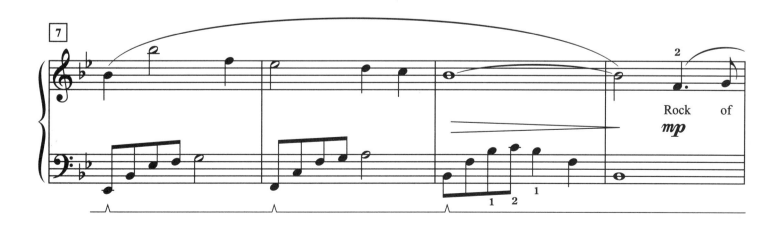

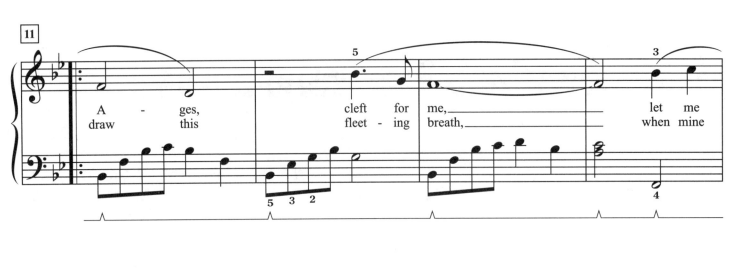

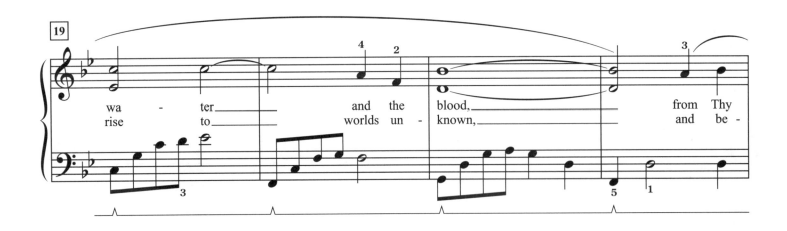

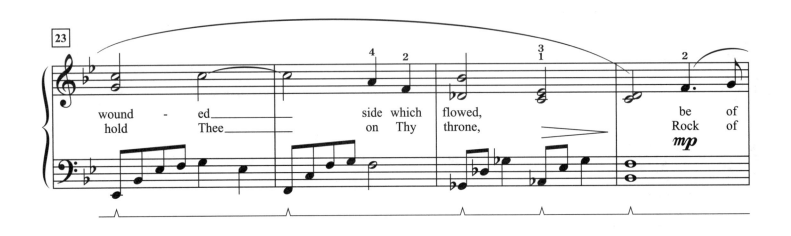

sin the
A - ges,

dou - ble cure,_____
cleft for me,_____

save from
let me

wrath hide
my - self in

and make me pure.
Thee.

mf

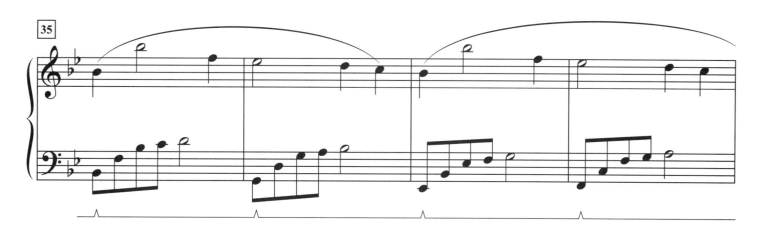

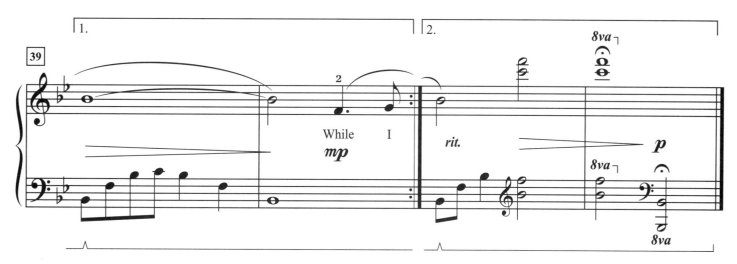

While I
mp

rit.

p

Simple Gifts

Words and Music by
Elder Joseph Brackett
Arr. Robert D. Vandall

turn, turn will be our de-light, till by turn - ing, turn - ing we come round right.

Sweet Hour of Prayer

Words by William Walford
Music by William B. Bradbury
Arr. Robert D. Vandall

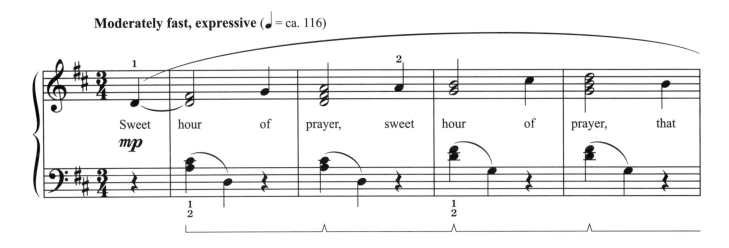

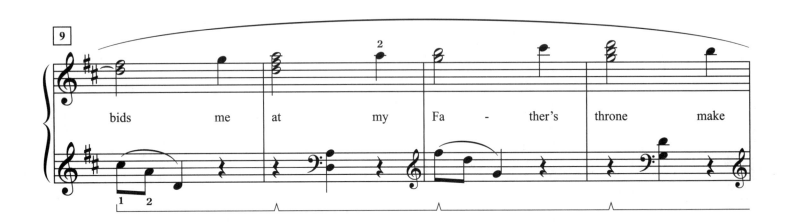

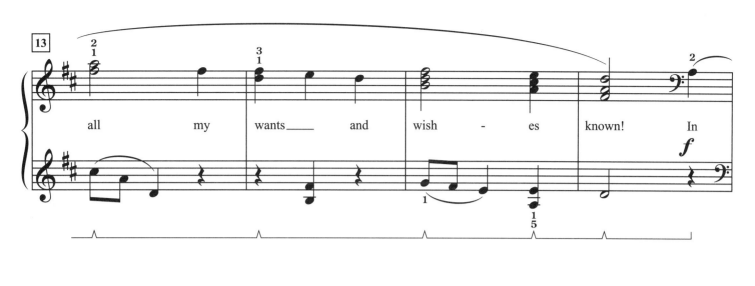

all my wants____ and wish - es known! In

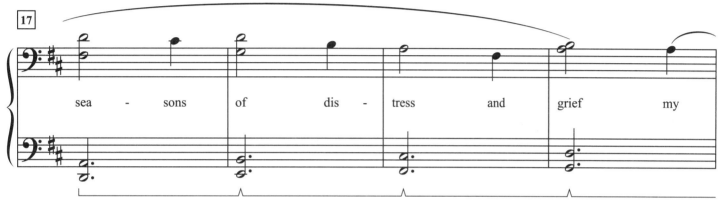

sea - sons of dis - tress and grief my

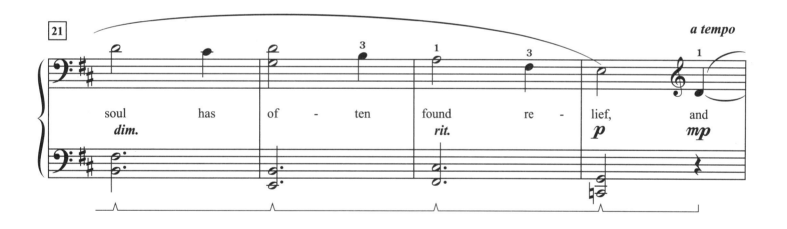

soul has of - ten found re - lief, and

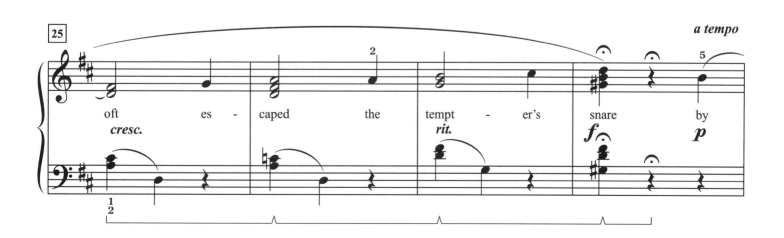

oft es - caped the tempt - er's snare by

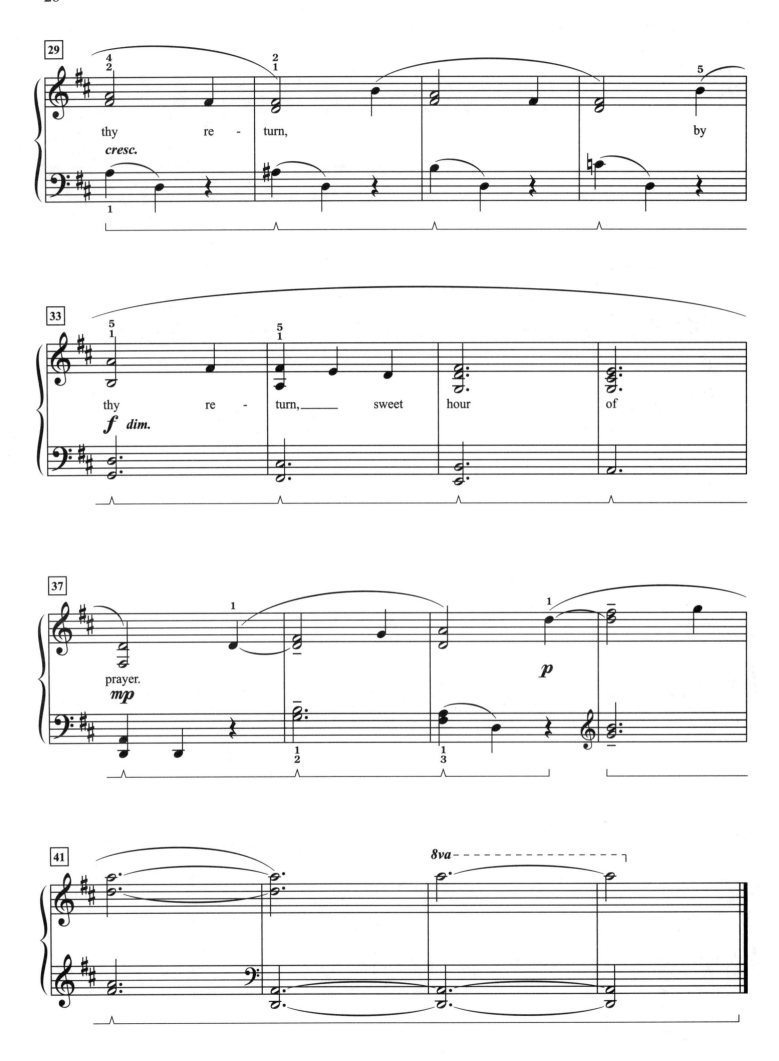

To God Be the Glory

Words by Fanny J. Crosby
Music by William H. Doane
Arr. Melody Bober

God be the glo - ry great things He hath done; so

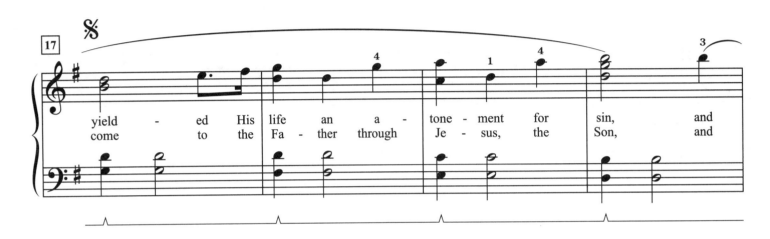

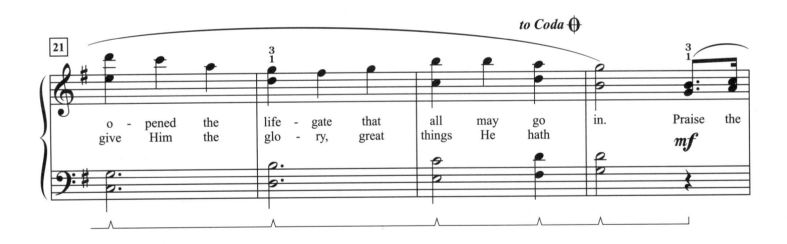

voice! Praise the Lord, praise the Lord, let the

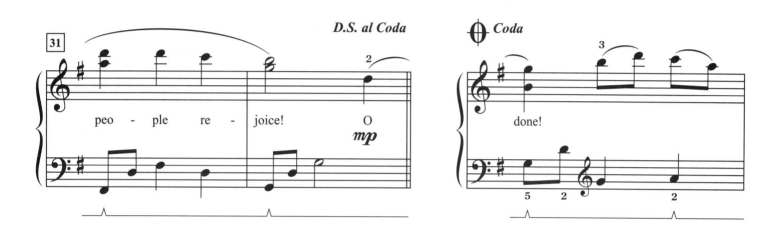

D.S. al Coda

peo - ple re - joice! O

Coda

done!

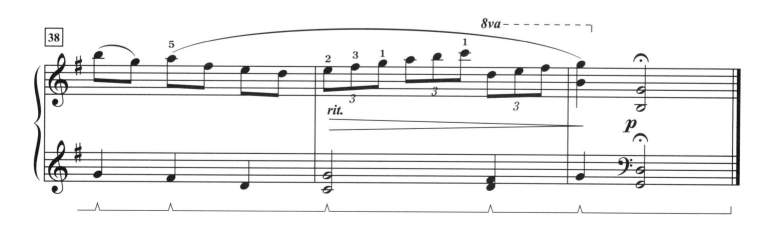

rit.

8va